Qis for Question

-An ABC of Philosophy-

BOOKS

Winchester, UK
Washington, USA

MW00990895

First published by O Books, 2009
O Books is an imprint of John Hunt Publishing Ltd., The Bothy, Deershot Lodge, Park Lane, Ropley,
Hants, SO24 0BE, UK
office1@o-books.net
www.o-books.net

Distribution in:

UK and Europe
Orca Book Services
orders@orcabookservices.co.uk
Tel: 01202 665432 Fax: 01202 666219
Int. code (44)

USA and Canada
NBN
custserv@nbnbooks.com
Tel: 1 800 462 6420 Fax: 1 800 338 4550

Australia and New Zealand
Brumby Books
sales@brumbybooks.com.au
Tel: 61 3 9761 5535 Fax: 61 3 9761 7095

Far East (offices in Singapore, Thailand,
Hong Kong, Taiwan)
Pansing Distribution Pte Ltd
kemal@pansing.com
Tel: 65 6319 9939 Fax: 65 6462 5761

South Africa
Alternative Books
altbook@peterhyde.co.za
Tel: 021 555 4027 Fax: 021 447 1430

Text copyright Tiffany Poirier 2009

Design: Tiffany Poirier
Production: Stuart Davies

ISBN: 978 1 84694 183 2

Printed by Tien Wah Press
www.chrisfowler.com

O Books operates a distinctive and ethical
publishing philosophy in all areas of its business,
from its global network of authors to production
and worldwide distribution.
This book is produced on FSC certified stock, within
ISO14001 standards. The printer plants sufficient
trees each year through the Woodland Trust to
absorb the level of emitted carbon in its
production.

Dedicated to My Students and Teachers

Author's Note

Welcome to the wonderful world of philosophy!

Since ancient times, famous thinkers like Socrates and Plato have investigated philosophy. Yet deep questions seek out everyone. They peak around corners. They pop into conversations. They dance around kindergarten classrooms.

Philosophy belongs to us all.

As a child, I would lay awake in bed at night pondering questions like, *Who am I? What is happiness? What is real?* Back then, I didn't know there was an area of academic study called philosophy. I only knew that thinking critically in this way made me feel more alive and enchanted by our mysterious universe.

Still looking for answers myself, I find that the very process of deep questioning adds a special meaning to my life. Perhaps you too are discovering the same.

If so, this book might come in handy. You could explore a page each day or week, ponder on your own, journal in the park, or debate with a friend. For more activity ideas, visit "Fun with Philosophy" at the end of this book or *www.qisforquestion.com*

I wish you all the best in your beautiful journey!

Sincerely,
Tiffany Poirier

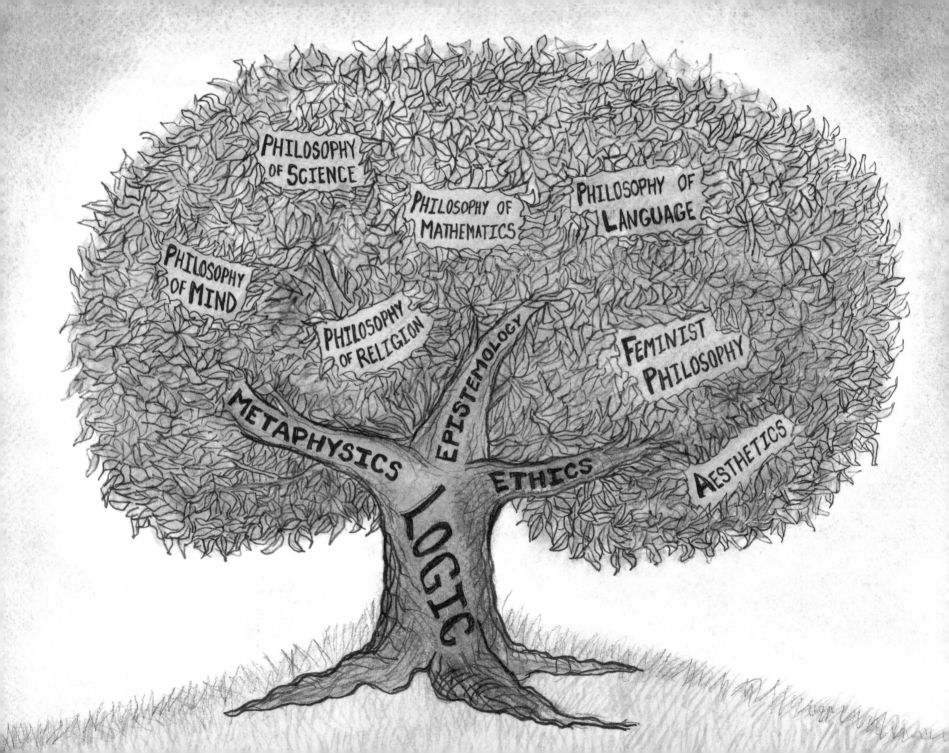

Answers

Searching for answers?
Let's begin!
How are they found?
Are they within…?

Beauty

To say something's "beautiful"—
What do we mean?
Is "beauty" an opinion?
Can it be unseen?

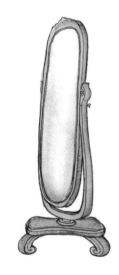

Cause

What was there
at the very beginning?
What caused the cosmos
to start spinning?
And in this universe so old and big,
which came first, the chicken or the egg?

Dreaming

Sometimes dreams
seem real,
And sometimes life
seems fake—
So how do you know
when you're dreaming?
How do you know you're
awake?

E

Existence

What is existence?
Can you define it?
Is there a boundary?
What is outside it?

At the edge of space,
if you poked your fist,
could you scoop in
your hand
what doesn't exist?

F

Free Will

Do you feel like
you're pulled by strings?
Is a puppet master
in the wings?
Did destiny plan
your life for you?
Or can you choose
the things you do?

God

What do you believe
of God?
What role
does your faith play?

If God called on the phone right now—
What would you want to say?

Happiness

What is happiness?
What is it worth?
Is pursuing happiness
our purpose on Earth?

Infinity

How deep is
deepest space—
How far does it
extend?
Does time move like
an arrow—
Will it ever end?

Justice

What is wrong? What is right?
Is justice more than black and white?
Who decides what justice is—
Is it those with greatest might?

K

Knowledge

How do you know
the things you know?
Is direct experience
the best way to grow?

And can we call knowledge,
a thought that's untrue?
*(Can you know the sky's green,
or that grass is blue?)*

$P \supset q$

$\sim q$

$\therefore \sim P$ } Valid!

If A, then B.
If B, then C.
∴ If A, then C.

?

A
C * B

No S is R

P	~P
T	F
F	T

Aa Bb C d Ee Ff Gg Hh Ii Jj Kk Ll Mm No

Logic

What makes an argument hard to tear down?
When is it valid? When is it sound?
What can we prove with logic alone?
Can logic reveal the world unknown?

And if all A's are B's, and all B's are C's,
then all A's are C's; don't you agree?

Mind & Body

Could a body survive
without a mind?
Could a mind ever leave
its body behind?

Nature vs. Nurture

Why are you the way you are?
Is it how you were raised?
Was it all in the stars?

Other Minds

If all you have felt
is your own consciousness,
can you be sure
other minds exist?
Are other people robots?
Are you a *solipsist?*

Solipsism: The philosophical idea that "My mind is the only thing I can be sure of that exists."

P

Possible Worlds

Of all possible worlds,
is this one the best?
If so, then why are there
conflicts and mess?

Do we need contrasts?
Do we need night—
To help us wake up
to the beauty of daylight?

Question

Do you question more now
than ever before?
Do the questions pile up
outside your door,
knocking so loudly
you cannot ignore?
Do questions bring questions…
and those just bring more?

Rights

What are your rights?
Are rights equal for all?
Which rights apply
to an animal?

Soul

Is there a soul?
Of what is it made?
Who gets a soul?
Do souls ever fade?

T

Truth

Should you always seek the truth,
investigating like a sleuth?
Can you think of an exception—
are there times we need deception?

And when truth appears before your eyes,
can you go on believing otherwise?

Utopia

Imagine a land
where all is ideal—
What is it like?
Could it be real?

UTOPIA

V

Virtue

What is noble?
What is good?
Can you always do
what you should?

Wisdom

When are you wise?
How do you know?
How does it feel?
How does it show?

eXamine Your Life

Is "the unexamined life not worth living?"
In your life, is something missing?
What parts of life should you dissect?
And what's the best way to reflect?

You

As you grow from day to day,
what parts of you will always stay?
Of what stuff do you consist?
And of this stuff
what will persist?

Zenith

What will be your zenith, your greatest success?
Will it be about money or whom you impress?
Will it be about all of the knowledge you possess?
What if there are answers you still need to guess?
Is your zenith a destination…
or a lifelong process?

FUN WITH PHILOSOPHY

Explore the big questions of philosophy through these fun activities and projects…

☑ QUESTION JAR

Hunt down exciting new philosophical questions and keep your collection on slips of paper in a special jar. Use these questions to inspire writing, discussion, and debating games with others.

☑ PHILOSOPHY JOURNAL

Start a "Philosophy Journal" to keep track of your ideas and beliefs as they evolve!

☑ PHILOSOPHERS' WALK N' TALK

Grab a question and a friend and head outdoors for a philosophical journey. See where the path and the conversation take you!

☑ POPSICLE STICK DIALOGUE

When discussing in a small or large group, use popsicle sticks to help keep track of speaking turns. Each person begins with the same number of sticks. A stick is tossed into a center pile after sharing an idea. This will inspire you to plan your words carefully.

☑ DIALOGUE WEB

Sit in a circle with a group of three or more people. As each person shares an idea, a ball of yarn is passed to him or her. The speaker holds onto a piece of the yarn and passes the ball to the next speaker…until the group has created a web of ideas!

☑ DEBATE

Put your arguments on trial! First, choose a topic (i.e. "Be it resolved that happiness is the most important thing in life."). Then, research, prepare and present your best arguments. You may want to brainstorm opposing arguments using an "Agree/Disagree" T-Chart.

☑ INVESTIGATE A PHILOSOPHER

Choose a famous philosopher to research. What did he or she believe, and why?

☑ START A "PHILOSOPHERS' CLUB"

Gather friends for regular debates and philosophical activities.

☑ HOST A "PHILOSOPHERS' PARTY"

Invite your friends to attend your party dressed up and ready to debate as their favourite philosophers. Increase the fun by focusing on a philosophical theme. For example, invite your friends "Socrates", "Plato", and "Aristotle" for an "Ancient Greek Philosophers' Toga Party."

☑ INVENT A GAME

Play around with your knowledge of philosophy by inventing your own *board game, game show, crossword puzzle*, or *quiz*.

☑ GET CREATIVE

Choose one or more philosophical ideas to explore through the visual, performing and language arts. Create a philosophical *drawing, painting, sculpture, cartoon, comic book, picture book, novel, newspaper, poster, billboard, magazine, essay, speech, poem, song, play, puppet show, radio drama, commercial* or *movie*.